WHOSE Comfort Zone ARE YOU IN?

How to lead the life you want and be happy every day!

Marilyn Sherman

**Stay Focused Seminars
Publishing Division**

Publisher: *Stay Focused Seminars*
               P.O. Box 125070
               San Diego, CA 92112-5070
               (800) 32-FOCUS
               (1-800-323-6287)
               Motiv8ter@aol.com

Author: Marilyn Sherman, Speaker & President, *Stay Focused Seminars*
Cover and Book Design gladly done by: Graphic Minion Studios • 619.676.6884

TABLE OF CONTENTS

ACKNOWLEDGEMENTS

I wish that I could thank all the people who I have ever met in my entire life, but since I can't, I would like to single out a few people who have made a significant impact on my life.

Clay Roberts - Thank you for your amazing encouragement to me when I was young (just a pup!). I want to acknowledge you for seeing the potential in me to become a trainer and speaker. I am indebted to you for giving me my first training job which jump-started my career.

Paul Jackson - You have been such a great coach. Even though I was never a wrestler or a football player, you taught me the values of hard work and integrity. I would like to thank you and your beautiful wife, Terry, for your friendship.

Doris and James Cassan - Thank you for your never-ending support and friendship over the years. Thank you also for providing me my first audience with your dedicated employees at Dollar Rent A Car.

Mike Dougherty - Thank you for taking the time to teach me the important values of being positive and believing in myself. You were a great, motivating teacher and your influence helped me to be who I am today. Thank you.

Mark Victor Hansen - Your enthusiastic support of me has been amazing. I'll never forget you sharing the platform with me at my very first National Speakers' Association event.

Jack Canfield - Thank you for your commitment and dedication to helping people. Your work in the field of self-esteem has influenced so many people and paved the way for many others.

Dr. Dennis Alimena - Thank you for being a mentor to me (especially when I lived in Allentown, PA). You taught me to have confidence in making decisions and to never look back. Thank you.

Dick Anderson - Thanks for being such an inspiration at my first seminar. You helped me to realize that I wanted to be a speaker and now I am one!

Lisa Schubert - Thanks for being my best friend, supporting me and calling me a star way before you ever heard me speak.

The late James W. Newman. - I never met him, but I had the pleasure of meeting his daughter Colby. Jim wrote the book *Release Your Brakes!* and he is the creator of the concept of the **Comfort Zone**. So, of course, I would like to honor his work and dedication to helping people and giving the world the concept of "The Comfort Zone."

And finally, I would like to acknowledge my family. To my parents and all of my brothers and sisters for your support and your patience. You have taught me so much, but most importantly, you all taught me that I could do anything that I wanted as long as I put my mind to it. Thank you.

I would like to dedicate this book to my sister Margie. Thank you for being such a great sister. Planting those beautiful gardens is only one of the many, many ways that you add so much love and joy to the world. Hold on to your vision of that spectacular ranch with beautiful horses and one day we will once again go riding. I love you.

What Is Your Comfort Zone?

"You have to be willing to step out of the pack and take risks, even jump completely out of your element if that's what it takes."

Carol Bartz

American Business Woman Chairman and CEO of Autodesk

"Life is a process of becoming, a combination of states we have to go through. Where people fail is that they wish to elect a state and remain in it. This is a kind of death."

Anais Nin, 1903-1985

French/American Writer and Lecturer

*H*ave you ever thought about your "comfort zone?" You know, that comfortable place where you live, breathe, and eat...your place of safety and security...the place where familiarity is like a warm blanket wrapped around you. It almost sounds great, doesn't it? It's not! When you live in your comfort zone, you may be safe and comfortable, but you're not growing or expanding your life experiences. Eventually, you become stifled, immobilized and discouraged.

Not uncommonly, people who are not satisfied with their lives, jobs or relationships prefer to stay comfortable in an unhappy situation because they don't want to risk the unknown. Fear keeps them in their ruts.

Let's take Sue, for example, an administrative assistant for a mid-size finance company who attended one of my seminars. "Marilyn, as a motivational speaker, I'm wondering if you can motivate me?" she asked.

"Tell me about your challenge," I said.

"I can't stand my job and I've been there for 17 years," she said.

"Have you ever considered getting a new job?"

"Are you kidding? I have just invested 17 years of my life in that job. How can I leave it now," Sue stated.

Her response was sad but all too common. Like others who attend my seminars, Sue is stuck in her comfort zone. Her job and paycheck are familiar aspects in her life. She knows there's something better for her or she wouldn't be asking. Yet, Sue is afraid to leave familiarity for the scary unknown. In this feeling, she is not alone.

Margo is another example of someone afraid to leave her comfort zone. For 2½ years, she had dated Bill, a man who clearly stated that he would never marry. Their first year together was filled with fun, romance and excitement. During the second year, however, Margo's values changed. She realized that she wasn't getting any younger, and marriage became more important to her. Furthermore, Bill wasn't Margo's idea of husband material.

Now, wouldn't you think Margo would drop Bill and find someone more suited to her values? Then, wouldn't Bill find another woman who wasn't interested in a long-term commitment? You may think this would be the way, but guess what got *in* the way? Their comfort zones. Margo and Bill were so comfortable with each other, it was easier to stay in their troubled relationship than to be single again (oh my!). They simply would not risk being alone while waiting for Mr. Right or Ms. Possibility to come along. For Margo, Bill was actually Mr. No-Way, Mr. Not-Even-A-Chance, but their comfort zones had such strong holds on them, they stayed in their relationship one-and-a-half years too long.[1]

Sadly, many abused women stay in the comfort zones of their

---

[1] By the way, after Margo made her final break from Bill, she immediately met a man who shared the goal of a committed relationship. Eventually, they married and lived happily ever after! Margo knows her wonderful new relationship would never have happened if she had stayed in her comfort zone with Bill.
"I finally took the risk of being alone, and in the end I got what I really wanted," she said.

troubled relationships because it's too hard to go out on their own and build a new life. Dr. Laura Schlessinger, author of *10 Stupid Things Women Do to Mess up Their Lives*, gives the response of one woman who is involved in her second abusive marriage. "At least this husband doesn't beat me as bad as the last one did." Do you see the pattern?

If you don't stretch your comfort zone, eventually your environment and/or relationships adapt to your old comfort zone. For example, let's take Joe, a 100-percent commissioned sales rep who makes an average of $2000 to $3000 a month. Joe has some very specific goals of being the top salesperson in his division. One month, however, he makes an incredible $4000 in the first two weeks. What does Joe do the last two weeks of the month? You're right; he slacks off! Unless Joe expands his comfort zone of earning an average of $2500 a month, he will play golf, sleep in, take a vacation, and make excuses for not going out on sales calls. The outcome, of course, is that he will go back to his established comfort zone without stretching into a new zone. Many times, Joe and other people like Joe don't even realize what they're doing.

The same barometer exists for your weight. Laura has worn size 16 for more years than she cares to admit. She doesn't like herself at her current weight and has been discouraged by her previous dieting attempts. When she discovered that her class reunion was coming up, she again decided to lose weight to fit in a size 12 dress. Laura dieted, worked out, eliminated high fat foods, and told her friends she was off Bailey's and Kahlua because she had to fit into her new dress. Lo and behold, Laura did it, and she looked spectacular in her new dress. In all, Laura enjoyed her new dress for about 15 minutes before going right back to her original lifestyle! Soon, she was back in her size 16 clothes.

Here's what happened: Laura didn't make any long-lasting lifestyle changes. She acted so drastically out of her comfort zone that instead of adjusting to the new lifestyle, she reverted back to her old ways... her old comfort zone, in other words.

Whose Life Do You Want To Live?

> *"Think wrongly, if you please, but in all cases think for yourself."*

Doris Lessing
British Writer

> *"Parents can only give good advice or put them on the right paths, but the final forming of a person's character lies in their own hands."*

Anne Frank, 1929-1945

$\mathcal{N}$ow that you understand the term "comfort zone," let's talk about the trap of getting into *someone else's* comfort zone. Keep in mind that lots of people haven't the slightest idea what they want to be when they grow up, even people who are well into their adult years. Others know what they want, but they've been so discouraged by other people, they don't attempt to fulfill their dreams.

Remember Whitney Houston's character in the movie *Waiting to Exhale?* After her longtime involvement with a married man, a man unavailable and unwilling to fulfill her needs, she broke off the relationship and moved to Arizona. One day, out of the clear blue, this Mr. "Already Attached" gave her a call, after getting her phone number from her mother. You see, her mother so wanted her daughter to be happy, she influenced her to let the man back in her life. Sure, Whitney's character could have been strong enough to follow through with her decision to break off the relationship, but it certainly didn't help to have Mom pushing her down a path she didn't want to go.

While the above example may be fictitious, there are plenty of people who move into someone else's comfort zone simply because it's a lot easier than stretching their own zones. It's especially easy when it is someone you work with, live with, or are married to. One reason it's easy to become pressured into living in someone else's comfort zone is because it relieves you of being accountable for your actions. You can blame your unhappiness on the person who was influencing you. In other situations, people try to keep you from risking and growing because of their own fears and insecurities, their own comfort zones. Have you ever told someone you were on a diet, and the next day they sent you cookies? Maybe this person didn't want you to succeed in losing weight because she wasn't successful in losing weight herself.

Here's a personal example. I will never forget attending my first seminar when I was only 17 years old. I attended Dick Anderson's motivational *"Self-Image Psychology"* program, where I learned to develop my own personal vision and mission for my life. So, at age 17, I decided that I, too, wanted to become a motivational speaker.

After reflecting on how I wanted to live my life, I decided upon my mission. I wanted to go out and speak to businesses around the world and motivate employees to improve their productivity by improving their self-images and self-esteem. I became excited now that I had defined my purpose. I wanted to motivate the masses, knowing that people who feel good do better work. Then, reality hit. For me to have credibility as a speaker in the business environment, I knew I would have to first get a job in a business environment!

After graduating from Washington State University, I spent several months pounding the pavement in Seattle looking for a job. Finally, my dad lit a fire under me by saying, "If you don't have a job within 30 days, you will have to move out of the house!" On the 28th day, I had a job.

My new job wasn't in the corporate world as I had anticipated, but it was a job. My mission of helping people feel better about themselves was just being fulfilled on a different level. I worked from midnight to 8 a.m. on a crisis hotline as a crisis counselor. After a few months, I realized this job wasn't fulfilling my ultimate mission, so I left and began working in my first corporate job with a finance company.

The corporate position was a great opportunity for me to work with all types of people. Eventually, I landed a position in the training and development department in Allentown, Pennsylvania. I spent several years researching, writing, and presenting personal and professional development programs, giving me the very experience I needed to become a motivational speaker on my own.

Finally, it happened. I had the opportunity to fulfill my ultimate dream when SkillPath Seminars in Mission, Kansas, asked me to audition for a training position. In this new position, I would travel around the United States and Canada, motivating the masses.

After hearing about my new opportunity, my father, the mentor businessman that he is, gave me a heart-to-heart, father-to-daughter talk. "Will you have a long-term contract with the company?" he asked.

"Like other seminar companies, they only offer month to month contracts," I answered.

"Will you have a guaranteed number of working days a month?"

"No Dad, there are no guarantees, no monthly minimum and no maximum."

"What about benefits?" he asked.

"As an independent contractor, I'm afraid the benefits come right out of my own pocket."

Dad decided then he'd better give it to me straight. "Marilyn, you're with a big firm and making good money now. The company has been in existence for many years. I recommend that you stay where you are in Allentown with your guaranteed salary and benefits."

Dad wasn't intentionally being negative. I took his advice as meaning: "Marilyn, I love you so much, I want you to stay where you are, a place where it's safe. My role as a father is to protect you, and I want to protect you from failures and setbacks." With further translation, he was probably saying, "I'm really uncomfortable with you taking this risk. I would feel so much better if you stayed in Allentown."

Had I chose to stay in Allentown, I would have been living in my Dad's comfort zone, not mine. Don't get me wrong; I love my father very much and respect him as well. Yet, I needed to follow my *own* path, my *own* passion, *my heart*...no one else's, even someone else's I love, like my Dad.

SkillPath *did* hire me, by the way, and because the job was 100% travel, I could move wherever I wanted. I left Allentown and moved to my goal destination—San Diego, California. By the way, my "safe" job in Allentown wasn't so safe afterall. The company was sold and everyone in the Allentown office was forced to move to another state or to find a new job. Some of my friends were still looking for jobs a year later. Since you can't count on job security, you might as well follow your dream! Thankfully, I didn't listen to my father out of some sense of loyalty, intimidation or fear. Can you imagine if I had? I would have been out of work, maybe moved to another state and still nowhere near my goal of becoming a professional speaker.

Anytime you act out or make a decision based on what someone else wants (his or her comfort zone, not yours), two seeds are planted. One is the seed of anger and the other is resentment. When these two seeds are nurtured with large doses of self-doubt, fear, or negative self-talk such as "I shouldn't have listened to him" or "What does HE know anyway," the blossom becomes an unhappy person stifled of growth potential. To take the analogy further, the weeds of negativity will take away your life because you're not living your own life; you are living a life is based on someone else's comfort zone.

Keep in mind too that not everyone will advise you because they want to protect you. Some people may be blatantly negative and say "Oh, don't go for that job, you'll hate it," "You're overqualified," "You're not experienced enough," "You'll hate the travel," or "You'll burn out!" Here's the true translation:

"Please don't leave and succeed. Stay down here in mediocrity with me. I'm threatened by you and your actions of bettering yourself. I don't have the courage to leave my unfulfilled comfort zone. I want company, so I don't feel so alone." My advice is: Don't just walk away from these people, *run like mad!*

Chapter 2 Exercise •

It's Your Life:

What do other's want you to do with your life?

_____

_____

_____

_____

What would you need to do with your life for someone else to be comfortable?

_____

_____

_____

_____

How would you feel if you lived your life according to someone else's comfort zone?

_____

_____

_____

_____

What do you want to do with your life?

_____

_____

_____

_____

How To Determine What To Be When You Grow Up

> *"The future belongs to those
> who believe in the beauty of their dreams."*
>
> Eleanor Roosevelt, 1884-1962

> *"I am a little pencil in the hand of a writing God
> who is sending a love letter to the world."*
>
> Mother Teresa, 1910-1997

> *"Far away there in the sunshine are my highest aspirations.
> I may not reach them, but I can look up and see their
> beauty, believe in them, and try to follow where they lead."*
>
> Louisa May Alcott, 1832-1888
> Author of Little Women

*I*n Chapter 2 I stated that many people have no idea what they want to be when they grow up. How does this happen? Many people are spending a lot of time trying to cram 24 hours of work into an 8-hour working day. Not only do they face daily challenges at work, but they are also dealing with family commitments and household obligations. It is difficult for them to lift their eyes off the daily grind to see which direction they are headed. Some people are so focused on their daily routines they don't realize the rut they are in, the rut that is created when they don't set long-term goals for their lives. In fact, some people probably spend more time picking out the color of a new car or deciding what to pack for vacation than they do in planning their lives.

Unfortunately, many of these people end up like Sue in Chapter 1. She was the woman who woke up after 17 years to realize that she was so invested in a job she didn't like, she couldn't possibly leave it. How about you? Are you climbing up the imaginary ladder of success only to find that the ladder is propped up against the wrong building?

Let's talk about how you can determine what you really want to be when you grow up.

Stephen Covey, best-selling author of *Seven Habits of Highly Effective People*, offers this suggestion: Imagine your own funeral. It is the end of your life (of course, you're at least 101!) and five people are speaking at your funeral, the glorious celebration of your life. These people represent various parts of your life: family, work, community, spiritual and/or religious affiliation, and your best friend. They have been asked to talk about you and what legacy you have left behind. As representatives from all areas of your life, they create a total picture of the life you led, and the significance you left. Who did you touch in a special way and how? What were your significant contributions? Now, Steven Covey suggests that you write out the script for these five people. I love this exercise...who would you pick? What would they say?

As a result of these scripts, you can create a life you would like to live. Certainly, none of your scripts would have said: "She was spectacular in living the life her father wanted her to live." Or, "She was the most average person I have every met. She did the same things all her life, never risking and never growing."

If picturing a funeral is too uncomfortable, then plan your 95th birthday, when a group of people are throwing you the party of a lifetime. Who will be there? Who will speak on your behalf? Imagine your grandchildren reciting their school papers entitled, "What my grandparent has meant to me and why." Maybe the newspaper is writing a story on the big bash. What highlight in your life would make the headline? Let's go one step further; imagine Hollywood making a movie out of your life and how you touched people in extraordinary ways. Think of a title for the movie... "Life Lived on the Edge" or "The Quiet Yet Rewarding Years" Or "One Life that Made a Difference for Many."

In another example, imagine that your favorite magazine is

doing a feature article on you with your picture on the cover. What would the headline be? What part of your life would be worthy of the article? Who would be quoted in the article? Now, write the article!

The object of these suggestions is to help you live the life *you* seek and to help you stretch *your* comfort zone. Stretch it to the limits; bask in the glory of planning your own life, not living it as others want you to.

As you reflect on these suggestions, don't allow negative beliefs to creep in. Release yourself from all negative thoughts about what wasn't or couldn't be possible; think only of all your dreams coming true. Brian Tracy, in his tape album *The Psychology of Achievement*, suggests that you imagine your goals as though neither time nor money were objects. Tony Robbins, author of *Unlimited Power*, says that your past does not equal your future. Eliminate the negative self-talk and imagine all the possibilities. Give yourself permission to be totally outrageous. Now, go write your story!

Scripts for your Funeral:

Best Friend: _____

Script: _____

_____

_____

_____

Work Rep: _____

Script: _____

_____

_____

_____

Family Member: _____

Script: _____

_____

_____

_____

Community Rep: _____

Script: _____

_____

_____

_____

Spiritual Rep: _____

Script: _____

_____

_____

_____

95th Birthday Party

Partial Guest List: _____

_____

_____

_____

Paper Title from grandkids: _____

What my Grandparent means to me: _____

_____

_____

_____

_____

Newspaper Headline: _____

Now, Write the story for the newspaper: _____

_____

_____

_____

_____

_____

_____

_____

_____

_____

_____

_____

Movie of Your Life:

Title: _____

Who would play you? _____

Now write the plot: _____

_____

_____

_____

_____

_____

_____

_____

_____

Magazine Article:

Name of Magazine: _____

Article Headline: _____

Now write the Article: _____

_____

_____

_____

_____

_____

_____

_____

_____

What is Self-Esteem?

"You cannot hope to build a better world without improving the individuals. To that end each of us must work for his own improvement, and at the same time share a general responsibility for all humanity, our particular duty being to aid those to whom we think we can be most useful."

Marie Curie, 1867-1934

Somewhere, somehow self-esteem has been given a bad name in some circles. When I speak to groups on the importance of self-esteem, people often interrupt to tell me that I'm teaching people to be self-centered and unspiritual. That couldn't be further from the truth of my message, so let me clear it up now.

Self-esteem is a combination of how you feel about yourself (your sense of worth) and how you see yourself (winner/loser, fitting in/not fitting in, lovable/not lovable, etc.). When you feel comfortable about yourself and confident that there's a place for you in the universe, you will have a sense of calm and acceptance. Not only will you feel an unconditional acceptance of self, but you will also feel an acceptance of others. When you feel you don't have to constantly prove yourself, that's when you are able to give unconditionally to other people.

Giving unconditionally means to give without need or intent of external validation. People with high self-esteem see external validation as a bonus because their true validation comes from within. When you reach the point of giving without expecting anything in return, I believe you have reached the epitome of spirituality. Having goodness flow from the inside out creates positive energy that influences other people. Others can't help but be inspired by your effervescence. Unfortunately, the beautiful radiant light that surrounds each of us is often clouded with self-doubt, insecurity, petty comparisons with other people, and negativity of the past, present or future. Furthermore, your radiance can be clouded by the *"If-Only"* or *"I Should Have"* games. Let's talk about these two games, which are so popular among pessimistic people.

"If-Only" Game

The *"If-Only"* game may be played by people from ages 10 to 100, individually, with a partner, or with teams. To qualify for the game, you must have a negative attitude and low self-esteem. Here's how the game works: You are stuck in your comfort zone, your familiar yet unfulfilled life. You cannot move up and out because you don't have what it takes. So, the object of this game is to stay immobilized in your comfort zone by naming all the reasons why you can't move.

☆ *If only* I had more: confidence, credibility, composure, courage, money, education, time, friends, experience. . .

☆ *If only* I had less: debt, worries, problems, insecurities, commitments, responsibilities. . .

☆ *If only* I were: older, younger, single, married, with children, without children, thinner, heavier, taller, shorter, prettier, plainer, healthier. . .

The only way to win this game is to quit playing it! For each of the above excuses, there are others who have those exact same challenges. Yet, they chose not to play the game and moved up and out. These people had enough love for themselves and others to get out of their potential misery and make a success of their lives.

"I Should Have" Game

Similar to the *"If-Only"* game, the *"I Should Have"* game is played by looking negatively into your past or looking dimly into your future. Both are equally effective in sabotaging your self-esteem and keeping you in your comfort zone.

☆ **Looking into the Past** - *I should have*: gone to school, stayed in school, stayed single, told my mom how I felt before she died, started my diet last month, spoken up for myself, stayed home, gone back to work, gotten married, gone to graduate school, been nicer to my pets, written more letters, paid my taxes sooner, told my dad how I felt, written that book, let go of my anger, followed my dreams...

☆ **Looking into the Future** - *I should be*: more like Susan, more happy, more wealthy, thinner, doing better than I am, married by now, more disciplined, more responsible, more organized, more spiritual, more giving, a better parent, sister, friend, neighbor...

Again, like the *"If-Only"* Game, the *"I Should Have"* Game has no winners, only losers. Therefore, be careful not to get caught up with playing either one of these games. If someone else wants you to play, please realize there is nothing to gain from playing. In fact, people who are constantly playing the *"If-Only"* and *"I Should Have"* games are people who generally have low self-esteem. They are also good recruiters getting others to play their game.

Let's take a closer look at the word "should." Think of how you feel when someone says, "You know what you should do." The question is, for *whom* should I do?

The word "should" is associated with a set of rules, such as "you should stay home with your children the first five years of their lives." According to whose rules? Or, "You should marry someone who is the same: race, religion, age range."
According to whose rules?

Incidentally, each of us has our own set of rules. We can change them, modify them, and embrace them. The only thing we can't do with our rules is to expect other people to know, understand, accept and abide by our rules. In fact, conflicts in relationships occur when one party expects the other party to understand his or her rules.

After a recent speaking engagement in Seattle, I had lunch with one of my college roommates. I asked her if she had a nice Valentine's Day. "It was great, but one day my husband is going to send me roses instead of carnations," she said.

"Have you ever told your husband that you wanted roses?" I asked.

"No, but he should know that without my telling him," she said in the classic of all replies.

I'll bet I can second-guess my friend's set of rules:

"Good husbands should know their wives' desires."

"Good husbands should read their spouses' minds."

"Good husbands should give what their wives want without them asking."

Maybe my friend thinks it might sound too demanding or controlling if she asked for what she wanted or needed. Her rules, however, make her sound judgmental, don't they? And, she's really not!

This example explains why you feel resentful, defensive, angry, shameful or guilty when someone tells you what you should do. The "shoulds" are based on rules, and rules are enforced by judges. The judge, of course, is whoever made the rules. Therefore, we judge or we are judged when we don't follow the "shoulds". You can now see the pattern that emerges when you follow someone else's rules, which are based on his or her own comfort zone.

Let me offer my solution. Eliminate the word "should" from your vocabulary. If you want to offer advice, use the non-judgmental, empowering word "could." For example, "Here's what you could do."

When someone chooses to give you unsolicited advice, say "Don't should on me!" Over the years, I've conditioned my sister Margie, so she now says, "May I make a suggestion?" rather than "You know what you should do." I'm certainly more open to hearing her suggestions than I am to hearing her tell me what I should do. Besides, if I don't like her suggestion, I can always say, "Thanks for your contribution."

People with high self-esteem are not directed by other peoples' sets of rules as I was a few years ago. I used to think that everyone else's needs came before mine. In fact, I wore a button that said, "I'm Third," meaning God was first, other people second, and me third. Unfortunately, I tried so hard to meet everyone's needs, I became a "people pleaser."

A people pleaser takes on the responsibility of caring for other people's needs and wants. As a people pleaser, I believed that someone's unhappiness or sadness was somehow my fault and I needed to fix it. I became accommodating, submissive, and ever-changing to make all other people happy. Guess what happened? My self-esteem waned so much, I became confused as to whom I really was. In addition, I was so exhausted from saving the world one person at a time, I allowed anger and resentment to grow inside. I became unspiritual as I adapted to everyone else's comfort zones and their sets of rules.

Eventually, I learned how to take into consideration my needs before others, thereby giving me the capacity to give others unconditional support. I learned to love myself enough to set boundaries based on my own rules. I became committed to my boundaries and knew I was worthy of standing up for myself if any of those boundaries were violated.

Today, I don't have to absorb someone's negativity such as anger, or a bad mood, and make it my fault. I will support that person unconditionally as long as he or she doesn't violate my boundaries by yelling, using abusive language or acting improperly. Then, I'm able to walk away with my self-esteem in tact. I also recognize that I am worthy of having supportive people in my life who respect my boundaries. So, when I say "no" to a request, I know people will not be offended and pressure me into compromising my position.

Before you start thinking I've taken a selfish outlook on life, let's look at this analogy. Whenever you are on an airplane (any airplane and any destination), you will always hear the safety instructions sounding something like this:

> *Ladies and gentlemen, in the event of loss of air cabin pressure, an oxygen mask will come down in front of you. If you are traveling with a small child, put your own mask on first, then help the child who cannot help himself.*

With my old way of thinking, I would have made sure that everyone on the entire airplane was wearing their oxygen masks, and I would have died. What good would I be spiritually or otherwise if I was dead?

Give to yourself first, then you will have the capacity to give unconditionally to others. That's when you have self-esteem.

Marilyn Sherman

Your Boundaries & Self-Esteem:

What boundaries have you allowed others to invade? _____

_____

_____

_____

_____

What boundaries would you be willing to work on out of love for self and others? _____

_____

_____

_____

_____

What would be a situation that might come up that would threaten your self-esteem? _____

_____

_____

_____

_____

How are you going to respond to these potentially negative situations if they ever occur again? _____

_____

_____

_____

_____

Whose Comfort Zone Are You In?

CHAPTER 5

_H_ow To Get Self-Esteem

"Remember no one can make you feel inferior without your consent."

Eleanor Roosevelt, 1884-1962

"You can't give people pride, but you can provide the kind of understanding that makes people look to their inner strengths and find their own sense of pride."

Charleszetta Waddles, 1912

American Nun and Writer

$\mathcal{Y}$our self-esteem will be brought down when you try to do too much and when you feel obligated to please people just so they will like or accept you. When you try to be all things to all people, you end up in someone else's comfort zone, which could be a negative one. And don't forget how living in someone else's comfort zone creates anger and resentment.

No matter how positive you are, negative people find ways to try to bring you down. Some will lure you down with gossip; others will discourage all your good ideas.

Think back to a time when you were excited about a new job opportunity or another exciting event in your life. Maybe a negative person began questioning your judgment. Possibly someone advised you not to go for the promotion because you didn't have enough experience. In another example, maybe you told someone your intentions of joining a health club. Rather that supporting you, this person may have suggested that you would soon lose interest and end up wasting your money.

Negative people attempt to bring you down to THEIR level, because that's where they are comfortable. Furthermore, negative people who have low self-esteem are threatened when it appears you may be improving yourself. They won't admit this to you; in fact, they may not even admit it to themselves.

Negative people love to give unsolicited advice. Remember the line I use when people give me unsolicited advice... "Thank you for your contribution." As an example, I remember one woman who attended my *Time and Stress* seminar. After the seminar, she came up to the podium to tell me that I had taken a potentially boring topic and made it dynamic and fun. That part was fine and dandy, but then she launched into her unsolicited advice: "I just want to tell you one thing that would change your credibility immediately. Just between us girls, you REALLY need to cut your hair to shoulder length and dye it dark black!"

She wasn't the first seminar participant to obsess about my hair. I have heard all types of suggestions for new styles, colors and lengths; everyone has an opinion about my hair. I simply thank these participants for their contributions. I thanked this woman as well, even though she was insistent on telling me I would be more credible to wear my hair as she suggested. I didn't allow her to change my self-esteem. In fact, I use that as an example in my assertiveness seminars. I tell participants if I were a negative, aggressive person, I'd probably be overtly offended and make a comment about her hair. If I were passive with low self-esteem, I'd probably go cut and dye my hair!

To keep your self-esteem and confidence, avoid people who bring you down and focus on connecting with positive people. When you meet "negative dream busters" (whom I call toxic), replace them with people who are supportive, positive and understanding. Have you ever met someone and it didn't take long for you to feel the energy drain out of your body? On the other hand, have you ever connected with someone and it felt as if you've known them forever? Be very intentional about who you spend time with. Complete the next exercise which will help you think about people you know. Then you can make decisions on who you choose to spend time with.

Toxic people to avoid:	Positive, helpful people to surround yourself with:
_____	_____
_____	_____
_____	_____
_____	_____
_____	_____
_____	_____

What brings you joy? What makes you laugh? Take a few minutes and think about all of those things that make you feel good. Remember the last time you felt goose-bumpy good? Think about the time you were blissfully happy or pleasantly content. Think about what you were doing that brought so much joy and happiness in your life. Now make a list of what you were doing:

_____

_____

_____

_____

_____

_____

_____

_____

_____

_____

_____

_____

_____

Go back over your list and write down when you last did each activity. Begin creating goals for yourself so you can follow through on doing those things that make you happy and do them more often. Don't forget the simple things either, such as:

☆   Walking on the beach

☆   Reading a good book

☆   Riding a horse

☆   Roller blading

☆   Laughing hysterically

☆   Sending funny cards to long-lost friends

☆   Taking a long, hot bubble bath complete with candles

☆   Lounging on a comfy couch and reading a magazine from cover to cover without guilt.

The list is endless!

Once you have created a list of things that bring you joy and happiness, think about what you can do for other people. When you do something to brighten someone's day or to make them feel good, you can't help but feel good yourself.

If you are stumped about what you can do for others that will make you feel good, here's a great starter list:

☆ Volunteer your time to a shelter for abused women or children.

☆ Clean out your closet and take everything you haven't worn in a year to a shelter or non-profit thrift store.

☆ Collect all your hotel shampoos and soaps and make care packages for a shelter.

☆ Take your neighbor's dog for a walk.

☆ Send a "thank you for being my friend" card to another person.

☆ Call people you have lost contact with; let them know how much you appreciate them.

☆ Initiate a "Clean-up the Community" event.

Now, make your own list of everything you can to for someone else "to make his or her day:"

_____

_____

_____

_____

_____

_____

_____

_____

Another great way to raise your self-esteem is to keep a "win list." Keep track of all your wins during the day. My experience tells me that if 99 things go right during the day and one thing goes wrong, you will end up talking about that one wrong thing over dinner.

When you keep a win list, you condition your brain to keep track of the good things; in turn, you consciously begin to remember the good things in your day. Some people call it a gratitude list because you end up writing down things that make you grateful. As you keep your win list, don't write down any negatives. Reflect on only the positives, such as a nice compliment someone gave you, a nice message you received, or a pleasant exchange you had with someone during the day.

I like to keep my win list in my Day Timer. Then, whenever I get down, which thankfully isn't often, I reflect back on my wins and I suddenly feel much better. Your list ends up being a great attitude adjuster.

You can do the same thing with a humor file. Keep track of all the things that make you laugh. You know you need a humor file if you've had anyone come up to you and say "smile, it's not that bad!" Hey, in this potentially stressful world we live in, we need more humor! Besides, you cannot laugh hysterically and be stressed out at the same time! When you keep track of all those things that make you laugh, then at any given point in your stressful day you can take a reprieve and read your humor file. My humor file includes an incident that happened to me in Alaska. A woman I met in Fairbanks told me: *"I've lived in Alaska all my life, so I want to tell you something. There are SO many men in Alaska that the odds are good. But I must warn you, the goods are odd!"*

The next day I was speaking in Anchorage. As I walked into the seminar I kept thinking to myself, "The odds are good, the goods are odd." Then, I said "Good Morning" to the audience and welcomed them with open arms. What I didn't expect was the button on my blouse to pop off! I completely exposed myself to that group of men in my seminar! I can laugh at the incident now because it really was funny. Of all the places for me to expose myself!

When you keep track of the funny things that happen, then at any given moment in your day, you can laugh and get your endorphins flowing. Endorphins are natural chemicals in your brain released into your system to give you a natural high sensation. Endorphins are released after vigorous exercise, sex or hysterical laughter. This is good news. The next time someone asks you to work out with him or her, just laugh hysterically and say, "I don't need to!"

Make a list of all the people in your life who are positive or who you appreciate:

_____ ⋮ _____

_____ ⋮ _____

_____ ⋮ _____

_____ ⋮ _____

_____ ⋮ _____

Now, give them a call or send a note to say how much you appreciate them.

Win-List Starter Kit: Start your win list now. Write down all the great things that have happened in the last week:

_____

_____

_____

_____

Humor File Starter Kit: Think back on things that made you laugh hysterically? Write those things down:

_____

_____

_____

_____

Hopefully you will have to continue both of your *Starter Kits* on a separate sheet of paper! Go ahead!

Whose Comfort Zone Are You In?

*H*ow To Set Goals for a Happy Life

"If I had one wish for my children,
it would be that each of them would reach for goals
that have meaning for them as individuals."

Lillian Carter, 1898 - 1984

Mother of President Jimmy Carter

"We all live with the objective of being happy;
our lives are all different and yet the same."

Anne Frank, 1929 - 1945

*I*t amazes me how few people have written down their goals. When I ask people who attend my seminars what their goals are, most haven't even thought about them. Yet, if you read about the most successful athletes, business people, entrepreneurs, and actors, they all have one thing in common: they have written down clear-cut, specific goals for themselves.

Many people get bogged down in the details of how they will accomplish their goals. They usually don't know how to go about meeting their goals, so they give up even before they start. In this chapter, you will learn the "Four Musts" for goal setting.

Must #1: Be Outrageous

The first "must" is to be outrageous. Be limit-less! Begin your goal-setting session as if you have access to a magic wand. If you could wave your magic wand right now and have anything you wanted in life, what would it be? Remember, there are no stipulations when you have a magic wand; that's what makes it magic.

If you had unlimited resources of time, money, equipment, experience what would you do? What would you do if you knew beyond a shadow of doubt that you would not, could not fail? Imagine that you have all the assurance and confidence in the world, what would you do? Dreaming big is empowering and exciting.

Authors Jack Canfield and Mark Victor Hansen wrote of an inspiring story in their book, *Chicken Soup for the Soul* (Volume I, Page 191). Fifteen-year-old John Goddard sat down and wrote at the top of a piece of paper, "My Life List." He then proceeded to write down 127 goals. At the time the book was printed, he had achieved 108 of them! Some of his amazing goals included climbing the world's major mountains—Mt. Kilimanjaro, Mt. Kenya, the Matterhorn, Mt. Rainier and Mt. Fuji. His list also included amazing explorations and accomplishments such as learning the complete works of Shakespeare and learning French, Spanish and Arabic. And, the list goes on!

If you become stuck in your goal-setting progress, follow Mark Victor Hansen's suggestion of taking 20 minutes to write down 101 goals. Allow yourself to write without judgement and see what comes out. This is called "free-flow writing." Let your imagination and creativity run wild. Let all of your dreams, aspirations and passion flow out of you and on to your paper. Once you have completed this step, you can move on to the next must.

Must # 2: Be Specific

Make sure you complete "Must #1" before you begin this step. Your brain is one of your greatest resources. In fact, as soon as you state a goal, your brain acts like a heat-seeking missile. It will search out the most direct path until it hits the target. At the base of your brain is a reticular activating system, which filters out information that's not important to you. As soon as you set a goal, specific information that will help you achieve your goal goes through your subconscious mind to your conscious mind.

For example, let's say you approach the salesman at a car

dealership and express your interest in a new car. You are a unique and special person, so you don't want just any new car; you want one that will stand out from all the rest. The dealer sees the excitement in your eyes and says, "Boy, do I have the car for you! It's a purple Cadillac and it's unique and special just like you!" You are excited and impressed, and more importantly, to the salesman, you are sold. The next thing you know you're out on the open road in your new purple Cadillac and guess what happens? You see another purple Cadillac, then yet another!

You are angry and confused. Did everyone just go out and buy a purple Cadillac? No, they were out there already; you just didn't notice them because it was unimportant information.

Think about it...haven't you been in traffic before, daydreaming, when suddenly you see "your car" with someone else driving? It's not literally your car, of course, but it is the same make, model and color. Out of all the cars going by in traffic, you spot yours. Coincidence? No, your reticular activating system is at work. This same process works when you set your goals.

Set specific goals for yourself so your brain can support you in attaining them. Your brain won't stop until your goal is achieved, so make sure that it is something you really want.

Let me give you an example of writing a specific goal. If your goal is to make more money, state exactly how much money. When you're ambiguous rather than specific, your brain will swing into action to find ways for you to make more money. However, if you find a $5 bill, your brain will quit searching for more money!

You can accomplish your goal when it's stated in a specific manner. Then, your brain will continue to feed your conscious mind with ideas, creativity and strategies to help you fulfill your goal.

Jack Canfield, in his tape series *"How to Build High Self-Esteem,"* tells the story of how he was making $17,500 a year. His goal was to earn $100,000 a year, so he made a creative, but imaginary, $100,000 bill and placed it above his bed. He saw this sign every night and every morning. From that point on, he became creative in selling his speaking engagements, books and other people's books. That year he made approximately $93,000. He didn't meet his goal of $100,000, but $93,000 was much better than $17,500!

Must #3: Visualize Your Goal

Once you are specific about what you want, then you must be able to picture yourself as if you have already attained it. Because "Must #3" is vital in successful goal setting, it will be covered in more detail in Chapter 10. Of course, you will truly have to believe that your goal is achievable, or you will be subject to self-doubt and soon other people will be doubting your ability to achieve it as well.

Once you visualize it, you can believe it because it becomes your reality. I have my parents to thank for this one. They instilled in me at a young age to act as though my goal had already been attained. I will never forget an incident when I was in the fourth grade. My dad gathered all of my bothers and sisters, my mom and me around our kitchen table one night after dinner. We occasionally had these structured "family meetings" to discuss different issues affecting the family. This particular night, he had gathered us around to discuss plans for an upcoming vacation he was planning. He announced that we were renting a motor home and driving to South Dakota. Being the positive goal-oriented person that I was, I used Must #3 without even realizing it. I raised my hand (we had *formal* family meetings) and when my dad called on me, I asked with all sincerity, "If we go away on vacation for two weeks, who will take care of my horse while we're away?"

I will never forget my dad's response. He knew how desperately I loved horses and bless his heart, he gently reminded me, "Marilyn, you don't have a horse." I was so far into believing that I would get my horse, I truly was concerned about leaving it while we went on vacation. I didn't have a horse that year, but I persisted until my belief became my reality the following year. I then spent 10 glorious years riding and showing horses with my sister Margie.

One way to visualize your goals as if you have attained them is to cut pictures out of magazines. Gather pictures of things you want to do, places you want to go, people you want to surround yourself with, cars you want to drive, houses you want to live in, and recreation you want to participate in.

Gather pictures that represent all areas of your life, including physical, spiritual, vocational, personal and social. Once you have your pictures, place them on a poster board and write affirmations relating to each picture. For example, one of my goal boards has a picture of a woman riding a beautiful horse on a beach. My affirmation below the picture says, *I enjoy visiting my sister's ranch and riding horses yearly.* This represents one of my goals to help buy my sister a ranch where I can come visit and ride horses with my nieces and nephews.

When you write your affirmation, make sure it is a positive statement. Write what you want, rather than what you want to avoid. For example, I have a few physical goals represented on my goal board. One picture I have is of an extremely athletic, healthy woman working out. My affirmation states: "With a daily workout routine, I attained and maintained my goal weight."

You may be tempted to write what you want to avoid: "I will stop eating peanut M&M's." "I will stop smoking." "I will not be disorganized." Your brain doesn't comprehend the negative, so it will focus on peanut M&Ms, smoking and being disorganized. You move toward and become what is uppermost in your mind, so make sure your focus is on what you want rather than on what you want to avoid.

Must #4: Share Your Goals Selectively

Your goals are personal and it takes courage to identify them, to believe in them, to write them down, and to publicly declare them. The last thing you need is to have someone burst your bubble of enthusiasm with his or her negativity. For this reason, be careful with whom you share your goals. Certainly you won't want to share them with the negative people you listed in Chapter 5. Share your goals with only those people who will be supportive. Take time to find positive people; they're out there. You will soon see who is supportive and who isn't.

If you converse with someone who has a sarcastic, negative attitude, limit how much information you disclose. Instead, search out people who are positive, people with a healthy outlook in life. Surround yourself with people who will support you unconditionally. I can't emphasize enough how important it is for you to avoid negative people who can derail your plans for success, causing you to live in someone else's comfort zone rather than your own.

Incidentally, you don't have to personally know positive people. Zig Ziglar, in fact, was a big influence on my life. I listened to his tapes while I was in high school and college; I appreciate how his philosophy was an influence on how I chose to live my life. Recently, I wrote him a letter and expressed those feelings. Much to my surprise he wrote back. Now I have connected with one of the most positive people I know. Who would you like to connect with? Who would you like to surround yourself with? Make a list and write them a letter.

Goals and Affirmations

Remember, when you write your goals, write some for every area of your life so you have balance.

What do you want?	Affirmations: Write a positive statement as if your goal is already attained.
Dream Goal:	Affirmation:
Physical Goal:	Affirmation:
Relationship Goal:	Affirmation:
Spiritual Goal:	Affirmation:
Work-related Goal:	Affirmation:
Monetary Goal:	Affirmation:
Miscellaneous Goal:	Affirmation:

CHAPTER 7

Recognize Your Choices

"I have learned from experience that the greater part of our happiness or misery depends on our dispositions and not on our circumstances."

Martha Washington, 1732-1802

Former first lady of the United States

"Choosing Healthy Options Increases Chances of Excellence and Success.

CHOICES"

Marilyn Sherman

Speaker, Author

"You don't get to choose how you're going to die, or when. You can only decide how you're going to live. Now!"

Joan Baez, 1941

*I*f you look at the word "CHOICES," you will see the acronym—Choosing Healthy Options Increases Chances of Excellence and Success. Successful people, who I define as winners, are happy, accountable, living in the present, optimistic about the future, and most importantly they are people who constantly accept that life is filled with choices. Life is a choice; happiness is a choice. The best way to illustrate this powerful concept is to look at stress. What stresses you out? What makes you tense? What causes you anxiety? Make a list:

_____

_____

_____

_____

_____

_____

Surprise... those were all trick questions. Nothing stresses you out! Guess what? You stress yourself out. Stress is the result of you sending messages of danger or fear to your brain. The interesting detail, however, is that you can send those messages when there is real danger, such as an oncoming train while you are stuck on the track, or when there is an imagined event, such as you *visualizing* yourself stuck on a track with an imaginary oncoming train. Your physical response is identical whether the event is real or not.

Your stress is determined by your reactions to events in your life. Yet, when people are asked about what stresses them out, most will answer traffic, too much work, not enough time to do everything, crowds, weather, canceled flights, paying taxes, debt, deadlines, and teenagers.

Keep in mind...nothing can stress you out because stress is not tangible. Stress is a physical manifestation that originates from a thought. For example, let's say you set out to drive from San Diego to Los Angeles on Friday at 3 p.m., an interesting choice of day and time, but it's your choice. The traffic is horrendous, so your typical two-hour drive is now going to be three and one-half hours. Does the situation itself cause stress? No! It's your point of view, your attitude, and your interpretation of the facts that determine your stress.

Someone with a busy schedule and negative attitude would visualize the bumper to bumper traffic, the tie-up at the I-5 and I-805 interchange and curse at the stupid schedule, becoming more hot and bothered with each thought about the drive ahead. In fact, this type of person is usually stressed and anxious before he or she even gets into the car.

Now, let's look at a healthier option. Person #2 has a full schedule, but she uses her time wisely. Due to choices she has made, Person #2 acknowledges the challenging time of day to leave San Diego, accepts it, then searches for an opportunity in the situation. She celebrates the opportunity of having three or more hours of uninterrupted time to listen to motivational tapes or Spanish tapes. (She wants to speak fluent Spanish by the time she retires in Cabo San Lucas!)

Person #2 constantly studies positive successful people and success strategies, continuing on a daily path of unlimited learning and growing. She knows that the more she learns, the more she earns; and, the more she knows, the more she grows.

Picture both drivers in the line of traffic. One is miserable, uncomfortable, unhappy, and probably experiencing a few physical effects. The other driver is likely relaxed, smiling and taking in the scene, probably without any negative physical effects at all. Remember, it is not the traffic that causes your stress; it is your interpretation of the traffic—time delays, crowded lanes, obnoxious drivers—and your attitude toward it that determines your stress.

I often explain this scenario during my seminars, and when I mention the part about teenagers causing stress, someone inevitably says, "You don't have teenagers, do you?" No, I don't, but my favorite response is, "Imagine you didn't have them anymore." I know this a hard reality for many to accept, but when you change your perspective, you change the way stress affects you.

Let's say your teenager has a 10 p.m. curfew and it's now midnight when you receive the telephone call every parent dreads. "There's been an accident; please come to the hospital immedi-

Marilyn Sherman

ately." The ride to the hospital is filled with anxiety. In the absence of information, you think the worst. When you arrive at the hospital, you see a circle of your child's friends; then thankfully you see your teenager alive and well.

Yes, there had been an accident. A drunk driver ran a stop light and hit the car your child was driving. Unfortunately, the drunk driver was seriously injured and both cars totaled, but the occupants of your child's car were not seriously hurt.

On the way home, your teenager explains that he became the designated driver so his friends who were drinking would not have to drive themselves home. Think of the gratitude and relief you would feel. Just maybe you would say, "I love you so much. I don't know what I would do if anything happened to you." And, maybe your teenager would respond, "I love you too, and I promise I won't do anything to make you worry like this again." This is what's commonly known as a wake-up call. Unfortunately, we don't always take time to tell our family and friends that we love and appreciate them until something drastic happens.

I want to tell you about a touching letter I received from a woman who attended one of my seminars. She had lost her son when he was only four years old. In her letter, she thanked me for helping her put her son's death into perspective. She explained that after listening to my seminar, she decided to let go of her feelings of anger, hurt and loss over the death of her child; instead, she would focus her energy on being grateful that her precious son had graced this earth for four years. Remember, stress is all about perspective. I don't ever want to minimize the devastation of losing a loved one. But I do want to remind people that we all have a choice. Is the proverbial glass half-full or half-empty? You always have choice and I believe the healthy choice is obviously to focus on the positive.

On another occasion, when I was speaking at State College Pennsylvania, the registrar slipped a message to me that a seminar attendee had received an urgent call from her husband. As I usually do when this happens, I handed the woman her message and said, "Hey, you may have just won the lottery!" With a blank look on her face, the woman scurried out of the seminar to make the call. I reminded the audience that in the absence of information, most people think of the worst case scenario; someone must be hurt, something has happened to their child.

With those dreaded thoughts bouncing through your mind, imagine your state of mind if this happened to you. You rush to the lobby where you discover that all the pay phones are in use with people standing three deep to make their own calls. Then as you dash to the front desk, the power goes out! What is your physical response going to be? Increased heart rate...sweaty palms...tension in your neck and shoulders...tightness in your throat...short, heavy breathing...clenched fist, jaw and brow. You would probably scream at this point.

In the case I mentioned, the phones were not occupied and

there was no power outage. When the woman returned, I asked if everything was alright. She said, "Oh, my stupid husband! He had won tickets for a Steve Miller Band Concert in a radio call-in contest, and he was too excited to tell me later!"

The point to the story is...don't waste undue energy by worrying over that which you do not know or that which is out of your control. You actually cause unnecessary wear and tear on your physical and mental state. Just imagine your body having to adjust to roller coaster emotions and physical reactions every time you get stressed. It's hard work for your body to normalize after a sudden surge of adrenaline is pumped into its system. Your body has to slow down your heart rate, relax your jaw, normalize your blood pressure, release the adrenaline that has been pumped into your system, and re-relax your muscles. If your body has to do this every time you choose to look at situations as stressful, it eventually takes a toll on your body.

Another reason not to put your body through emotional and physical changes is the effect on your immune system. Your immune system keeps you from getting sick. If your body is constantly adjusting and re-adjusting to stress, your immune system becomes weak and you become even more susceptible to illness and disease.

Now, here comes the biggie! If your stress contributes to you being sick, and your stress is determined by your attitude and perception of a situation, and you alone control your choices in attitude and perception, (drum role, please...) then *your health is ultimately your choice*. Here are some choices to think about when confronted with a potentially stressful situation:

☆ Choose to have a healthy outlook.

☆ Choose NOT to panic about the unknown or things over which you have no control.

☆ Choose to remain calm until you have all the facts.

☆ Choose to look for the positive in any situation.

People with positive outlooks and positive mental attitudes live longer than those who don't. Furthermore, they also recover quicker from sickness than their negative counterparts.

What should you do when you are confronted with a potential stressful situation? Here is a suggestion:

BREATHE! - If an event is potentially stressful, make breathing your first and foremost automatic response. People who are confronted with a threatening situation commonly forget to breathe, thereby depleting their oxygen supply. Have you ever said, "I'm so stressed out I can't even think straight?" Taking deep breaths while you gather more information and analyze your options will help you remain calm and composed. As calmly as possible, think about your choices and their consequences.

I could choose to:	*And get:*
Scream and yell ☛	A headache
Act out violently ☛	Arrested
Talk it out ☛	Clarity and resolution
Ask questions ☛	A reality check

ANGER - Let's take a closer look at anger. Certainly, it's okay to be angry in many situations. But, what you do with your anger may not be okay. It is good to ask yourself, "Is it really worth it if I choose to lose my cool right now?"

Have you given yourself permission to be angry? Some people grew up in environments where it was unacceptable to express anger. Unfortunately, when these people become adults, they experience the inevitable feelings of anger, then they feel guilty or ashamed of their angry feelings. Now the original feeling of anger is compounded by additional destructive feelings. These new destructive feelings may lead you into sudden outbursts of hostility and violence; internally, they may produce physical affects such as an ulcer.

You don't have to feel guilty or shameful for feeling anger. It is how you express your anger that may not be healthy. For example, if someone offends you in some way, do you want to lash out and hurt them? Is it really worth it? Let's look at an example.

I flew to San Diego from the East Coast late one Friday night after a long travel schedule and sleeping in a different hotel room every night for a week. After several flight delays and missed connections along the way, my plane finally landed at 2 a.m. By the time I picked up my luggage and took a cab to my car, it was 3 a.m. I climbed into my car to head home with one thing on my mind—sleeping in my own bed. While waiting at a stop light, I noticed a pick-up truck filled with teenagers facing me in the opposite direction, and judging from the sounds coming out of the truck, the group had been out partying. When I began to make my right-hand turn, the driver of the truck immediately ran the red light to cut me off. I was angry. I wanted them to know it too. So, in my anger, I laid on my horn, and it felt good!

Was blowing my horn a good idea? **No!** The driver skidded to a stop, put his truck into reverse, and started backing up into me. I quickly put my car into reverse so I wouldn't be hit by the truck, praying no one was behind me. Thankfully, the truck stopped, then it proceeded ahead of me down the street.

I sat in my car, gripping the steering wheel with white knuckles, and thought about my various options. I didn't know any other route home, so I took a few deep breaths and proceeded forward. As I rounded the corner, I could see the pick-up truck parked perpendicular across my lane, and the teenagers were getting out of the truck with baseball bats. I was so frightened, I blew passed them, crossing a double yellow line and running a red light to get on the freeway towards home before they could jump back into the truck and follow me. I have never felt as panicked as I did at that moment.

Was my anger justified? Of course. Was it wise to honk my horn to show my anger? Of course not. Postponing your angry reaction may be the route to survival, especially on today's freeways. In a phenomenon known as *road rage,* people no longer hit their high beams to show their anger when you change lanes without signaling or when you drive too slow in the fast lane...they shoot you!

Letting your anger out is healthy, but safety comes first. Make sure you are in a safe environment where you can express your anger without fear of escalating an argument or having someone retaliate. In looking back at my 3 a.m. fiasco, I could have let the pick-up cut me off, took a few deep breaths, shrugged it off, then when I was in the safety and privacy of my home, I could have expressed what jerks they were.

One way to handle your anger and stress more effectively is to change your language:

Change language from:	To instead be:
I have no choice ☞	*I always have choices.*
I have to go to work. ☞	*I choose to continue working so I will receive a paycheck to support myself and my family.*
I have to leave this marriage. ☞	*I believe my safety is paramount, so I choose to leave this unhealthy relationship.*
I have to go. ☞	*I have a prior commitment, so I'm leaving now.*
You make me so angry! ☞	*I am angry that you didn't follow through with your commitment.*

Stress and You:

Look at the list of things that you said stressed you out in the beginning of this chapter. Now make a list of more positive reactions you could have to each one. Remember, it's about CHOICE and PERCEPTION.

Things that previously stressed you out:	*New, empowering perceptions of those things:*
_____	_____
_____	_____
_____	_____
_____	_____
_____	_____
_____	_____
_____	_____
_____	_____
_____	_____
_____	_____
_____	_____
_____	_____
_____	_____
_____	_____
_____	_____
_____	_____
_____	_____
_____	_____

Marilyn Sherman

Recognize Your Efforts

"If you have made mistakes, even serious ones,
there is always another chance for you.
What we call failure is not the falling down,
but the staying down."

Mary Pickford 1893-1979

*H*ow do you feel at the end of your day when you realize you didn't finish everything on your to-do list? Do you recognize your efforts? Those things you did accomplish? Or, do you focus on what was left undone? By the way, when was the last time you completed everything on your daily to-do list? Can't remember? You're not alone. If you are like most people, your daily to-do list is longer than the number of hours in a day.

Here's a good way to take a reality check. Write down items for your to-do list, prioritize them in order of importance, then determine how long it will take to complete each item. Total the time, then compare it with the amount of *discretionary* time you have. *Discretionary time* is the time which you have control over. In other words, it is time you can use at your own discretion. *Non-discretionary time* is the time taken up or influenced by other people.

As an example, if you own your own business which employs a small staff, you probably wear different hats during the day: receptionist, troubleshooter, marketeer, and sales executive, to name a few. The majority of your day is probably spent in *non-discretionary* time. However, if you are a research analyst with six months to complete a project, you probably have lots of *discretionary* time.

The key to remaining positive, not getting stressed, and recognizing your efforts, is to be realistic in setting your daily goals, so you don't become discouraged at day's end. It is important to develop the habit of accepting what you can and can't accomplish in a certain amount of time. Many people overcommit to what they can accomplish in a day. As a result, they don't get their work done and then they feel bad. So, don't start off with an unrealistic amount of work to get done each day. Then at the end of your day, you can recognize what you did accomplish. Just as you learned to focus on your daily wins rather than what went wrong during the day, you need to focus on the things you either accomplished or attempted to accomplish rather than what didn't get done. By focusing on the positive accomplishments, you will be giving yourself encouragement, which gives you momentum to continue and to maintain positive self-esteem.

Think about how you feel at the end of the day when you don't get everything done. Most people feel guilty or ashamed. These feelings are negative, self-destructive and harmful. Now is the time to change your focus!

When people plan their day, their schedule and their commitments, they often forget about their non-discretionary items. I met a woman who told me she couldn't plan her day because half of her day was taken up with meetings, phone calls and interruptions. She had 50% of her day as discretionary and 50% as non-discretionary. So I suggested that, if she worked a typical 8 hour day, she make sure her "To-Do" list did not exceed her discretionary time. In her case, this would be four hours.

Let's determine how much time *you* use for *non-discretionary* activities. How much time do you spend on the following activities?

Non-Discretionary Items:	*Time Spent*
Talking on the phone	
Attending meetings	
Chatting with drop-in visitors	
Dealing with unexpected, unplanned events	
Traveling to appointments/meetings off-site	
Other daily activities	
*	
*	
*	
*	
*	
*	
*	
TOTAL TIME SPENT DURING WORK DAY:	

Total all the time you spend on these activities. The total would be your *non-discretionary* time. They key is to make sure your *discretionary* items added to your *non-discretionary* items DO NOT EXCEED the total number of hours you are at work. For me, working out my own home office, the above non-discretionary items add up to approximately two hours. If, however, you work in an office with a staff and constant telephone interruptions, your non-discretionary time will likely add up to more than two hours.

Look at the patterns in your day. How much time does it take to do your job and at the same time handle interruptions, phone traffic and drop-in visitors? What about emergencies? Now that you have calculated your non-discretionary time, the time you have left is called your discretionary time. That's the time you have left to fulfill all your commitments and daily goals, your to-do list.

When you write your daily to-do list, estimate how long it will take to do each item. If the total time of the things on your to-do list does not exceed your discretionary time, you are being realistic. However, if your to-do list exceeds it, you are starting your day behind schedule and with undue stress and anxiety.

SAMPLE TO DO LIST (DISCRETIONARY ITEMS) Specific Tasks for Today:	Estimate of how long it will take to do:
1. Send press kit to Assoc. of Professional Secretaries	30 minutes
2. Prepare handout for Clemson University	1 hour, 40 minutes
3. Meet w/ Accountant about taxes	1hr, 15 minutes
4. Pick up dry cleaning	20 minutes
5. Prepare overheads for next week's seminar	20 minutes
6. Send thank you to D.A.'s office for booking seminar	10 minutes
7. Call Dave Morton and set up phone meeting	5 minutes
8. Pack for Speakers' Convention	45 minutes
9. Analyze con. agenda & choose sessions to attend	20 minutes
10. E-Mail BZ Betsy new names for membership in NSA	5 minutes
Total Time	5½ hours

Now subtract the total time of this chart from how long you are at work. The remaining time will be available for your non-discretionary items.

When you learn to make sure your to-do list does not exceed your discretionary time, you will have taken a big step forward in relieving stress that comes with over-committing your time. Looking back at my to-do list, you will note that it will take five and one-half hours of time.

> 8 hour workday
> - 2 hours estimated non-discretionary items
> 6 hours left in my workday to accomplish my
>   "To-Do" List (Discretionary Items) that I've estimated
>   will only take 5½ hours!

If I calculate that my daily routine includes two hours of time spent on calls, meetings and drop-ins (non-discretionary time), and if I allow myself a normal eight-hour work day, I now have six hours to complete my to-do list with 30 minutes to spare. For me, it appears to be a realistic day for accomplishing my tasks with minimal stress.

You will stress out even before you start your day if you forget about non-discretionary items. Keep in mind, too, that at any given moment an emergency could disrupt your schedule.

By keeping track of how long it takes you to do your job, eventually, you will see a pattern begin to emerge. You will then have a gauge for realistic planning when you write your to-do list.

The best time to create your to-do list is at the end of the day before you leave your office. At that time, you will know what has been accomplished and what still needs to be carried over to the next day's to-do list. It is also the perfect time to celebrate your accomplishments by reminding yourself about all the work you completed. By keeping track of your accomplishments, your computer of a brain will default its memory to what you accomplished rather that what you didn't. This is why I called this chapter *"Recognize Your Efforts,"* not *"Beat Yourself Up for What You Didn't Get Done."*

YOUR To Do List: *Don't forget answering e-mail and faxes!*	*Estimate of how long it will take to do:*
Total Time:	
Non-discretionary Items: *phone calls, drop-in visitors, meetings*	
Total Time:	

To-Do List Total Time: _____

+ Non-discretionary Items Total Time: _____

TOTAL : _____

If you work for someone, I recommend that you keep track of your accomplishments and send a status report to your boss once a week. "These are the things I accomplished this week, and here is what I have on my plate for next week." Not only will your boss appreciate the information, but the report will help you focus on your results.

If you think about your to-do list, it probably includes things that you don't particularly enjoy doing. For those items, you will probably need an incentive to get them done. Build a reward system for yourself so you can literally recognize your efforts. I'll give you one of my favorite ideas.

Because I have set the goal of staying fit even with an extensive travel schedule, I have come up with my own incentive. First, I must say I love nachos and I have probably sampled them in every city in the country. In addition, I can't say that I love to work out, but I do know it's necessary for my long-term health and vitality. So, I have established a somewhat juvenile incentive for staying fit, but it works for me. Every time I work out for 35 minutes or more, I put a star in my Day Timer. Yes, a star just like the one your kindergarten teacher used as a reward for good work. Now, whenever I look in my Day Timer, I see all the star stickers and become encouraged at the progress I've made toward my goal. So...go get some stars!

Make a habit of not overcommitting!

Whose Comfort Zone Are You In?

Recognizing your Efforts

Think of some things you have not completed:

_____

_____

_____

_____

_____

Now, recognize your efforts for what you DID get done. List all the things you DID get done today:

_____

_____

_____

_____

_____

_____

_____

_____

_____

_____

_____

_____

_____

_____

_____

_____

Let Go of the Past

"The little white ball won't move until you hit it, and there's nothing you can do after it has gone."

Babe Didrikson Zaharis, 1914-1956
(One of the greatest women athletes;
1946 winner of the U.S. Woman's
Amateur Golf Tournament)

One way to ensure that you are living and growing within your own comfort zone, and not someone else's is to let go of things that may derail you. I am sure you've heard the saying, "Yesterday is history, tomorrow is a mystery and today is a gift which is why it's called the present." Yet, many people choose to live in the past, or worse, they blame who they are today on events that have happened in the past.

You probably know people who are unhappy with their lives and unhappy with their circumstances, yet they are unwilling to take action to change their circumstances. You hear excuses such as, "I have no choice; that's the way my father was." Or "That's the way I am. I've always been like this." What a ridiculous excuse!

I was teaching a course on getting organized, when I mentioned that one of the fallacies of being disorganized is that disorganization is hereditary. One Chicago man disagreed by saying, "Heredity does matter. My father was disorganized, his father was disorganized, I'm disorganized, and now my son is disorganized." Based on the title of this book, you can guess what that statement sounds like to me. You're right, a comfort zone!

I'm used to seeing this mess; I've always been around a mess, so I'm comfortable with a mess...a mess is my comfort zone! In actuality, the person might say, "I know this place is a mess. It's been this way for a long time. I'm not really comfortable with being disorganized, but there's so much to organize, I'm more comfortable staying in the mess than thinking about the over-whelming task of creating a new organizational system."

Your past does not equal your future. At any given moment, you can change your situation. Simply decide to take action and to make those changes. Remember the song *"Man in the Mirror"* by Michael Jackson? The song is about being accountable for your own actions and knowing that change begins with you.

Unresolved issues from your past may be setting up roadblocks for you; yet, you *can* do something about them. Try writing about these issues in your journal, talking to others, getting into thera-py, or joining a support group. Make a goal of exploring your past so you can move on with your life. In other words, look back in order to let go and move on.

I remember attending a support group for people with eating disorders and noticed that many of the people would attend the group for years. They talked about their challenges of compul-sively overeating and how they wanted to lose weight. Sadly, they have been telling the same stories for years. My question to them might be, "So what, now what?" It's as if they go to meetings to tell sad stories, but then don't do anything to change.

Some people have fears of intimate relationships because of old fears of being abandoned again. So what, now what? What action can people take to overcome this fear and let go of the past? Certainly, there are no guarantees about people and rela-tionships. However, if people continue to allow their fear of abandonment control them, they will neither get close to anyone nor allow anyone else to get close to them. For this reason, these people need to acknowledge their past relationships and to re-focus on the possibilities of now having positive, healthy, fulfilling relationships.

Even without guarantees, you can choose to take a risk, grow, then love and be loved. You are worth it! Past failures are not immobilizing for weight and relationship issues only. Hanging on to negativity from the past can affect all areas of your life.

One of my favorite stories of learning to let go involves two monks walking along a riverbank where they see a woman trying to cross the river. Without hesitation, one monk carries the woman across the river, then the two monks continue on their journey. Forty-five minutes later the second monk breaks the silence and asks the first monk, "You know our vows as monks prohibit us from having any physical contact with women. Why did you break that vow?" The first monk responds, "Are you still carrying her? I dropped her off over a mile ago."

What burden are you still carrying around from the past that prohibits you from enjoying the present; your gift, and looking to the future with hope and encouragement? Isn't it time to let it go and move on? One of the benefits of letting go is that you no longer have to harbor resentments from the past.

Speaking of resentment, let's take a closer look at it. Take a minute and recall a situation when someone said or did something inappropriate to you or to someone you love.

Resentment:

_____

_____

Rather than talking it out in a healthy way to resolve the problem and move on, you may have chosen to suppress it. When you suppress it, you're not dealing with it, so when you see or think about that person, your resentment, which is a close cousin to anger, seethes inside, eating away at you.

That is how resentment works. It will remain within you until you choose to deal with it and let it go. Let's say you are hurt by someone's inappropriate behavior, so you metaphorically put him in jail for punishment. You stand guard by the jail cell to ensure that he doesn't get out. Unfortunately, you don't realize that he has escaped out the back door, so whose really in jail? That's right, you are! Instead, why not choose to free yourself of anger and resentment and let go?

Here are a few suggestions for letting go:

☆ Write a long, detailed message of everything you want to say to someone who has done you wrong. Your message can be good, bad, or outrageous. Just let it free flow. After you have exhausted your thoughts on paper, rip it up into shreds.

☆ Find a rock the size of your palm. Begin massaging the rock, telling it everything in your heart and mind about the incident. After your rock has heard everything, go for a walk near a lake or countryside, then symbolically let go by throwing your rock as far as you can into the countryside or lake.

☆ Keep a journal and write everything out. Keep your journal in a safe place, then every so often, reflect back on your writing to see how much you have grown.

☆ Talk it out. If you can approach the person, with whom you are carrying resentment, with confidence that it will be a safe encounter, do so. If not, talk the problem out with an objective caring friend or a counselor.

● **Chapter 9 Exercise**

Letting Go of the Past

List all of the resentments you have including people you have resentments toward:

_____

_____

_____

_____

_____

_____

_____

_____

_____

_____

_____

_____

_____

Now, finish the following sentence.

I choose to let go of each of my resentments by:

_____

_____

_____

_____

_____

_____

_____

I choose to let go of each of my past resentments by looking at the positive. I am grateful for those incidents that previously caused me pain because:

_____

_____

_____

_____

_____

_____

_____

_____

_____

Whose Comfort Zone Are You In?

CHAPTER 10

$\mathcal{V}$isualize Your Success & Happiness

*"Keep your face to the sunshine
and you cannot see the shadows."*

Helen Keller, 1880 - 1968

*I*magine yourself five years from today. What are you doing? What does your job look like? What is your authority level? How are your work relationships? What does your business look like in terms of your success? What type of car do you have? What does your home look like? What are you doing for fun? Are your daily routines fun and enjoyable? Are you doing what you have always wanted to do? Now, PICTURE IT! Once you have set clearly defined goals for yourself, begin picturing yourself as though you have already attained them.

In order to stretch your comfort zone, you first have to visualize where you would like to be. For example, let's say you have a specific job promotion in mind. Start visualizing yourself in that position and already succeeding. Visualization helps you solidify your belief in yourself, thereby making it easier to obtain your goal. It becomes a self-fulfilling prophecy. First aim it, then claim it. Believe in it, then achieve it. You will start to exude confidence as though you had already met your goal. Then when you achieve your goal, you are more likely to stay there because it's now in your *newly-stretched comfort zone.*

Each time you stretch your vision, you are stretching your comfort zone. For example, when I applied for a training position at SkillPath Seminars, they sent me a plane ticket to come to their office for a live audition. I had approximately four weeks to prepare for the audition, so I immediately began visualizing my success. I surrounded my house with SkillPath flyers advertising the seminars I would be teaching; however, I doctored them up with affirmations such as "Presented by one of SkillPath's finest trainers, Marilyn Sherman." I also put affirmations in the form of responses from the audition on the walls in my bedroom and on my bathroom mirror: "You're hired! You're perfect for this job!" "When can you start?" I wrote them as quotes and signed them with the names of decision makers who would be at my audition.

I was mentally prepared for the audition on March 1, 1993. I opened with the following statement: "Welcome to the program. My name is Marilyn Sherman and as you know today's date is March 1, *1994*, and I have been a very successful seminar leader for SkillPath Seminars for one year now. In fact, it was exactly one year ago today that I interviewed for this job in this very same room when you hired me. Do you remember that day?"

The panel went right along with it and loved it. My audition went according to my visualization and afterwards they offered me the position. When you picture your success you become more confident in getting what you want and in feeling comfortable about keeping it.

You can also move your visualization from your head and place it in a physical format. You have already listed your goals in Chapter 6. Now, go through some of your favorite magazines and cut out pictures representing your goals, as I mentioned earlier. Remember to cut out pictures representing all areas of your life physical, spiritual, family, social and paste them up on a poster board with an affirmation to go under each picture. Now, hang your poster boards where you can see them. I keep my goal boards next to my bed; since I live alone, I'm not cramping anyone else's home decorating motif! I also travel frequently, so I took a picture of my goal boards and now carry a pocket version wherever I go.

Like I said earlier, we move toward and become what's uppermost in our minds. So, when you keep your visualization uppermost in your mind, you make it your realization.

I'll never forget an experiment I heard about from a motivational speaker at Mercer Island High School near Seattle, Washington. He told of an individual who was hooked up with electrodes to record his body movements. The facilitator of the experiment then walked the volunteer through the visualization of executing a perfect tennis serve. The monitor then recorded slight movements by the muscles needed to execute the serve. Even though the individual didn't look like he was moving a muscle, he visualized the serve and his brain sent the appropriate message to the body. Therefore, every muscle that's used to execute a serve was stimulated. You see, your brain doesn't know the difference between a visually imagined event and reality.

Every time you visualize your success or what you want to achieve, you are stretching your comfort zone. Then when reality hits, you are more comfortable with it. Be careful of what you visualize, however. For example, think about a time when you were asked to give a presentation and maybe how nervous you were. You stayed up all night before the event as you visualized the presentation; unfortunately, it wasn't a healthy visualization. You were probably thinking: *What happens if I forget what I'm supposed to say? What if my mouth goes completely dry? What if I trip on my way up to the podium? What if my mind goes completely blank.* I call this negative goal setting. Guess what happens? You are nervous so you do one of the things you pictured; you trip on the way to the podium. Then what do you say when you get up there? "I knew I would trip on the way up here. I knew that would happen."

Next time you're called to do a presentation try this: With every negative thought or visualization that seeps into your head, acknowledge that it is destructive and replace it with a positive visualization. You will be amazed at the results.

After you read through my sample visualization, create your own.

Name one thing you want to achieve:

My Example:

I want my book selected by the Oprah Winfrey Book Club.

Here's how I create the visualization for this achievement:

I am relaxing by my pool, reading my favorite magazine, "People," after traveling from a speaking engagement to a large travel association in Maui. My cell phone rings, and the person asks for me. After I identify myself as Marilyn Sherman, the voice explains that she represents Oprah Winfrey's Harpo productions and she asks me to stand by for Ms. Winfrey. I chuckle, thinking my best friend Lisa is pulling a fast one, when suddenly Oprah's voice snaps me into reality. Right away she says, "Yeah, it's me and I loved your book! When can you come to Chicago? I would like to do a special on changing the world through positive action, and your comfort zone book is perfect for us to spotlight." I laugh with excitement as she tells me that two first class tickets will bring me to Chicago if I am available in two weeks. I explain that I can't confirm a date without looking at my speaking schedule. Oprah agrees to call me back when I have my calendar in front of me. Before we hang up, she adds, "Are you ready for the world to know your work? As soon as our show airs, you'll be asked to share your motivational message with thousands of people, which could be very exciting." I have a huge smile on my face when I answer, "I can just picture it."

Now take the next step for yourself. Go to the next exercise and create your own visualization!

Chapter 10 Exercise ● ● ● ● ● ● ● ● ● ● ● ● ● ● ● ● ● ● ●

Create Your Own Visualization

Name one thing that you would like to achieve:

_____

_____

Now create the visualization surrounding it:

_____

_____

_____

_____

_____

_____

_____

_____

_____

_____

_____

_____

_____

_____

Don't wait; find some magazines and cut out pictures! Now hang them on the wall with your affirmations. Remember: *You move toward and become what's uppermost in your mind!*

Overcoming Obstacles

"There were angry men confronting me and I caught the flashing of defiant eyes, but above me and within me, there was a spirit stronger than them all."

Antoinette L. Brown, 1825-1921
First woman in the United States
to be ordained as a minister.

"We cannot expect in the immediate future that all women who seek it will achieve full equality of opportunity. But, if women are to start moving towards that goal, we must believe in ourselves; we must match our aspirations with the competence, courage, and determination to succeed."

Rosalyn Sussman Yallow, 1921
First woman to be awarded the Albert Lasker Prize
for basic medical research.

"You can't be brave if you've only had wonderful things happen to you."

Mary Tyler Moore

What are your obstacles? What keeps you from attaining your goals? What hurdles prevent you from being happy? Go ahead, list them here:

_____

_____

_____

Now, think about this...for every obstacle, there are people in the world who overcame this very same obstacle and went on to achieve great success. Let's look at some commonly discussed obstacles.

TOO OLD. Look at Mary Kay Ash. She started her multi-million dollar empire after her husband died and she knew she couldn't live off measly social security checks.

TOO YOUNG: Matt Damon and Ben Affleck, two young screen writers in their mid-twenties, recently received the 1998 Academy Award for Best Original Screenplay. They started writing "Good Will Hunting" as a creative writing assignment in college!

LACK OF FORMAL EDUCATION: Neither Tony Robbins nor Demi Moore graduated with formal high school diplomas; yet, they both achieved tremendous success in their chosen fields.

LACK OF MONEY: Michele Hoskins was on welfare when she turned her financial life around. She got ahold of her great-grandmother's recipe for syrup and is now a millionaire selling syrup to grocery stores and restaurants!

INSUFFICIENT TIME: This obstacle, which is really an excuse, has to go immediately. You hear it everywhere: *I don't have time* *to be organized, to put oil in my car, to work out, to go to school, to go on vacation...*and the list goes on and on. Guess what? I hate to break the news, but you have exactly the same amount of time as everyone else in the world. You have 60 seconds in a minute, 60 minutes in an hour, and 24 hours in a day, and so on. Time is a fixed asset that has to be spent whether you like it or not.

Eliminate the following two phrases from your vocabulary immediately: "I don't have enough time to do that" and "There aren't enough hours in the day." STOP! You do have time; but maybe you don't have enough time to follow through on everything you've committed to. Because you are accountable for your own time, try rephrasing your vocabulary this way:

☆ I haven't allocated enough time to do a quality job on that project.

☆ I have focused my energy in another area.

☆ I have chosen not to spend my time on that project.

☆ That project isn't one of my priorities.

Based on your new phrases, which show accountability, you can now do something about allocating your time, energy or focus. Recognize that you can't do anything about time, so it is unproductive to blame it. Instead, choose how and where you would like to spend the time you have.

Procrastination

Every time you procrastinate about something, there is a consequence. It may be good or bad, positive or negative, but there will be a consequence. For example, my to-do list included having a tune-up on my car, but I never seemed to allocate the time.

In fact, in my self-talk, I said, "I don't have time today for car maintenance." You can guess what happened next.

While driving from San Diego to Irvine for a speaking engagement one Sunday night, my car began slowing down on a deserted stretch of freeway near Camp Pendleton. The gas pedal wouldn't respond, the warning lights came on, and smoke began billowing out from the engine. I pulled over to the shoulder near a call box and became scared as another car pulled up behind me. I locked my doors immediately and called 911 from my cell phone. (You're right, I've seen "America's Most Wanted," not to mention "Real Stories of the Highway Patrol" and "Unsolved Mysteries.") The dispatcher instructed me to keep my windows rolled up, my seat belt on, and stay on the phone line. Now an interesting twist to the incident occurred. The man who had pulled up behind me quickly got back in his car and sped away after he saw me on the cell phone. (Moral...Get a cell phone and get your car serviced!). Luckily a friend I called came to my aid as well as a tow truck to bring me to safety. But, that was a scary, potentially dangerous situation. And, it could have been completely avoided had I made it a priority to have my car serviced. You are the only one in complete control of your day, so take control and make better decisions on how you allocate your time. Don't wait for important matters to become urgent before you take action.

When you put your life into perspective, you realize that you truly are blessed. If you complain about your job, as least you have one. If you complain about an abusive relationship, get out.

You are only a victim once, then you are a volunteer. If you focus on your obstacles, you will surely fail. If you see obstacles as challenges to grow and prosper, you will grow and prosper. Change your perspective because no matter how bad your situation is, it could always be worse.

Look around at your blessings and imagine what it would be like if they were gone. Study people who have had tragic lives; study how they overcame their obstacles. Read biographies about heroes, and read other people's amazing stories of overcoming obstacles, then your situation won't look so bad.

Chapter 11 Exercise •

Overcome Those Obstacles!

Take the obstacles you listed at the beginning of this chapter, then do your homework. Study successful people who have overcome obstacles, especially obstacles similar to yours. Then, change your focus.

List some of your heroes.	What obstacles did they overcome to become successful?

Now grab a sheet of paper and keep writing! What can you do now to overcome some of *your* obstacles?

$\mathcal{A}$ffirmations to
Keep You Happy Every Day!

"Expect trouble as an inevitable part of life and repeat to yourself, the most comforting words of all; This, too, shall pass."

Ann Landers

American Newspaper Columnist

*W*hat do you say when you talk to yourself? If you are like most people, 80 percent of the messages you send to yourself are probably negative. Keep track. Be acutely aware of what you are saying to yourself.

I teach a course on "Credibility, Composure and Confidence," and I am always amazed at one of the exercises I present. I ask the audience to imagine that they have low self-esteem, poor confidence, and an overall negative outlook on life. In that mode, I ask them to complete this sentence: "When I make a mistake I am _____." Regardless of the audience, the responses are similar. Typically, they say, "I am embarrassed, intimidated, angry, sorry, a loser, depressed, a failure," and my favorite, "I'm not surprised." After the exercise, I have the group shout, "Cancel, cancel," a technique I learned from Jack Canfield on how to cancel negative thoughts and replace them with positive ones.

Next, I ask the audience to imagine that they are positive, have great confidence, and healthy self-esteem. Then I ask them to complete the sentence: "When I make a mistake I can _____." The responses now are much more productive: "I can fix it, learn from it, laugh at it, celebrate my humanness, teach someone else so they don't make the same mistake, let it go, not beat myself up over it, admit it, and move on."

Watch your self-talk. In his book, *You Can't Afford the Luxury of a Negative Thought*, author Peter McWilliams states: "Positive thoughts (joy, happiness, fulfillment, achievement, worthiness) have positive results (enthusiasm, calm, well-being, ease, energy, love). Negative thoughts (judgment, unworthiness, mistrust, resentment, fear) produce negative results (tension, anxiety, alienation, anger, fatigue)."

Your thoughts determine your emotions, which in turn determine your actions. Only you are in control of your thoughts, which means you have more control of yourself than you think.

Do you know that there is a difference between positive and negative thoughts in their physiological effects on your body? The movie *Mask* with Cher demonstrates these effects. In the movie Cher's son, played by Erik Stoltz, has a defect which causes his head and brain to expand and bring on migraine headaches. Whenever he experiences severe pain, Cher holds him in her arms and facilitates a visualization. She asks him to go to his place of serenity. As he talks about the flowers, trees, and quietness, these positive responses eliminate the pain. Using positive affirmations cancel out the negative messages.

Imagine the power of your brain. When you do so, you will understand that you can't feed your brain with negativity. It will kill you. Stop right now! Replace your negative thoughts with positive thoughts. Remember that your situation could always be worse. Do you have a roof over your head? Do you have all your limbs? Do you have the mental capacity to understand the written word? Things are better than you may think. So, when something negative happens, remain calm and affirm a positive thought so you come out of the situation untarnished.

Technique for Remaining Calm

As discussed in the section on anger, there is one simple word that will help you remain calm. "Breathe." It's all too easy to jump to conclusions and fly off the handle when you are confronted with a negative situation. If you have ever "lost it," more than likely it was at the wrong time over the smallest little thing. For example, having a disagreement with someone that escalates to a confrontation. Before you say something that you may regret later, take a deep breath. When you breathe, you are buying yourself some time. The secret is to respond to the situation, but don't react to it.

St. Francis D'assisi said, "Seek first to understand, then to be understood." What does that mean? In simple terms, it means "SHUT UP!"

Listen carefully, then ask more questions. You're probably saying, "What if I can't think of a question?" (especially is it is a potentially "heated," emotionally charged conversation). Use the "echo technique" which means to take the last word the person said, then repeat it in the form of a question.

As an example, I'll use a story from one of my seminars in Torrence, California. After lunch, a woman in the front row began snapping her gum, making an annoying sound that resonated throughout the ballroom. During one of the breaks, a woman in the 15th row approached me and asked, "Marilyn, what do you say to someone who is snapping her gum?"

"I don't know," I responded. "It's annoying but I can't stop the seminar to address it. I am not comfortable with public confrontation; it really needs to be done in private."

The woman then decided to confront the other woman in private in the hallway. "Oh, you're the one with the gum. I can hear you all the way in the back," she said.

"Oh, I've had this habit since I was a kid," said the woman.

The first woman reported to me that the confrontation hadn't worked. At the next break, up came the woman with the gum to tell me about the confrontation. She explained that she wasn't offended about what the woman had said about her gum chewing. Rather, she was so shocked by the woman's statement that she simply came up with a quick excuse. She asked me what she should have said. I told her that she could have taken a deep breath, then asked a question. Here's how the conversation could have turned out:

"Oh, you're the woman with the gum. I can hear you all the way in the back."

(Breathe)

"All the way in the back?"

"Yeah, my friends and I can hear you. We think it is distracting."

(Breathe)

"Distracting?"

"Yeah, we can hear you and we are distracted from hearing Marilyn speak."

(Breathe)

"Oh, okay. Thanks for telling me." End of conversation.

You see, we sometimes disclose more information than we need to when we get anxious, nervous or upset. Take your time in conversations, especially when you are anxious. Think about what you are going to say before you say it. And, don't forget to breathe. Then, with more information, there is less chance for negative reaction. Make a habit of remaining positive and calm by using affirmations daily.

Affirmations

Affirmations are positive, empowering statements that you can recite to yourself. Even if they aren't true *yet,* they eventually will come true. When you add belief to your affirmations, you are stretching your comfort zone. Then you will constantly grow and live a more happy and fulfilled life.

When you get in the habit of using affirmations, it will be easier to remain calm when confronted. Here is a list of affirmations:

I am lovable and capable. • *I am talented.*

I contribute to the world. • *I am positive.*

I can handle stress. • *I am a good person.*

I make positive choices daily. • *I love to learn.*

I am growing daily.

I choose to send positive thoughts to myself daily.

I enjoy life. • *I feel great.* • *I love to give unconditionally.*

I am constantly stretching my own comfort zone.

I surround myself with positive people.

I love to be loving.

I'm comfortable with taking risks. • *I love to laugh.*

I see opportunities in obstacles.

I look for the positive in others.

Chapter 12 Exercise •

My Own Affirmations

Take two of the above affirmations, or create two of your own, and write them down on a 3x5 card. Place the card in your wallet, and three times a day take out your card and recite the affirmations 10 times in a row. Do this in the morning when you wake up, sometime in mid-day, then once again right before you retire for the day.

List below the two affirmations that you will then write on your 3x5 card.

Affirmation #1

_____

_____

_____

Affirmation #2

_____

_____

_____

Way to Go!

> *"You've done good. Give yourself a star!"*
>
> Marilyn Sherman
> Author, Speaker, Trainer & Publisher

*W*ay to go! Congratulations on completing this book. I hope you took the time to finish the exercises in the chapters. I would love to hear from you and how any of the suggestions in this book have helped you! You can contact me at:

Stay Focused Seminars
P.O. Box 125070
San Diego, California 92112-5070
1-800-32-FOCUS
(1-800-323-6287)
Motiv8ter@aol.com

Once you've read this book and experienced the difference it makes in your life, you may want to share a copy with a friend or two or three! I invite you to order additional copies to share!

OTHER PRODUCTS YOU WILL ENJOY:

"Go for the Goal" Live Presentation Audio Tape: *$15.⁹⁵*

Enjoy her energy as Marilyn Sherman shares practical ideas for how to set and follow through on your goals for the success that you want!

"How to Avoid Conflict Avoidance" Live Audio Tape: *$15.⁹⁵*

Would you do anything to avoid conflict? Marilyn Sherman guides you through this assertiveness training to help you face conflict, not avoid it.

"Whose Comfort Zone Are You In?" Books   _____ @ $14.95 = _____

"Go for the Goal" Live Presentation Audio Tape: _____ @ $15.95 = _____

"How to Avoid Conflict Avoidance" Audio Tape: _____ @ $15.95 = _____

Name:

Title:

Company:

Address:

City: State: Zip:

Telephone: Fax:

E-Mail:

Payment: _____ Check (please make payable to *Stay Focused Seminars*)

_____ Money Order

Order Amount_____ + Shipping Cost _____ = TOTAL _____
(CA Residents add 7.75% Sales Tax to "Order Amount")

TOTAL AMOUNT OF ORDER $ _____

MAIL TO: STAY FOCUSED SEMINARS
P.O. BOX 125070
SAN DIEGO, CA 92112-5070

Shipping & Handling
(USA: all others add $4 to each quote)

item total	shipping cost
1 item	$3
2 items	$4
3 items	$5

Larger quantity? Please call for a quote (800)323-6287.